Treasure

Daily Readings

Treasure
Program Components

The program presents a well-rounded stewardship program for use in sermons, worship, small groups, and at home. Components include:

Program Guide and Flash Drive
Instructions for planning and using the program, including sermon starters and discussion guides, worship videos, Leader Guide for small groups, stewardship campaign materials, commitment cards, promotional materials, and graphics.

Leader Guide (On flash drive and downloadable)
Everything needed for a leader to facilitate a four-week group study using the Daily Readings and DVD.

Daily Readings
Day-by-day meditations for personal and group use.

DVD
Casual, compelling talks by Jacob Armstrong on the weekly topics.

Leader Kit
One of each component.

"Where your treasure is,
there your heart will be also."
Matthew 6:21

Treasure

A Four-Week Study on Faith and Money

Daily Readings

Jacob Armstrong

Abingdon Press
Nashville

Treasure: A Four-Week Study on Faith and Money
Daily Readings

Jacob Armstrong

Copyright © 2014 by Abingdon Press
All rights reserved.

ISBN 978-1-4267-8198-8

14 15 16 17 18 19 20 21 22 23—10 9 8 7 6 5 4 3 2 1
MANUFACTURED IN THE UNITED STATES OF AMERICA

Contents

Week Three: Giving Your Treasure Back to God

Week Four: Don't Worry 'Bout a Thing

Introduction

At the first mention of the word *treasure*, my mind is filled with images of pirate ships, deserted islands, and an *X* that marks the spot. I think of a hidden chest filled with gold medallions, rubies, and diamonds. Treasure is something you search for, fight for, and go great distances to find. Treasure can bind people together or create division between those who once were close friends. Treasure can become the focus of your life. It can consume you. Treasure can be hidden and hoarded, or shared and enjoyed.

Whether we realize it or not, we all have treasure. We all have things we are searching for, fighting for, and storing up. Though the items in the chest are different, we all have treasure that holds great value to us.

Often we think our treasure will follow our heart. But Jesus, in his Sermon on the Mount, suggested the opposite—that our heart will follow our treasure. In his Sermon on the Mount, he put it this way: "Where your treasure is, there your heart will be also."

It is no wonder, then, that many of us feel a sense of disappointment about our lives and finances. We want to give our lives to our church, our family, our God. Instead, our heart follows our debt, our job, and our bills, and we haven't even realized it. As a result, we're left feeling conflicted and empty.

Jesus cared about our heart, so he taught about our treasure. *Treasure: A Four-Week Study on Faith and Money* will help all of us consider what we are giving our lives to. We will explore where we want to be investing and where we really are investing. We will experience together the power found in making God our treasure.

Treasure was developed for Providence United Methodist Church in Mount Juliet, Tennessee. Providence was a two-year-old church that had reached many who before had felt disconnected from God and the church. We realized that if we were to be like Jesus, we would have to care about our hearts, which meant we would have to talk about our finances! As a growing church, we also had financial needs and dreams. We felt that a traditional stewardship campaign would not be the most effective way to help new Christians see the need to give. It seemed that if we made appeals to give based only on the need to fund programming or even out of duty to the church, we would miss much of our audience.

We found in Jesus' Sermon on the Mount a beautiful way to talk to people about their finances and their need to give. We began by asking ourselves two questions:

Where do I want to invest my treasure?
Where am I really investing my treasure?

We learned that our answers to the two questions were often quite different. Not surprisingly, we also found that our hearts indeed were following our treasure, no matter how much we wished they were following our intentions.

As we considered how to change where we were investing our treasure (time, money, energy), we found that our hearts were filled with excitement and a growing sense of contentment. We studied the words of Jesus from the Sermon on the Mount, and our church experienced an amazing season of growth. A number of people made life-changing decisions about their treasure, and those decisions had transformative effects on the way they lived and gave. Giving increased significantly and continued to go up following the campaign. More than that, lives were changed. Young families tithed who had never even heard the term before. Retirees viewed their investments differently and began to reconsider the impact their treasure could have on the world, for God's kingdom.

Jesus taught about our treasure because he cared about our hearts. His words from the Sermon on the Mount still hold life-changing power today. His words show that God has more for us than what can be earned on a paycheck. God has treasure.

How to Use This Book

This book of devotional readings is designed for use by individuals and groups. However you are using the book, you will enjoy and benefit more from it if you follow a few simple practices.

The book is divided into four weekly sections of seven devotions each, to create a twenty-eight-day journey. At the beginning of each week, you'll be given a Scripture reading from Matthew 6, which is part of Jesus' Sermon on the Mount. Read the passage at the beginning of the week, and then *reread the entire passage each day of the week.*

After rereading the weekly passage each day, move to the daily devotion. You'll find that your focus will be sharper if you set aside a specific time and place. Before you begin the devotion, take a deep breath and settle in. Allow these moments with God to become a part of your life rhythm. If you miss a day or two, don't give up! Just jump back in.

The daily devotion consists of a Scripture, written reflection, and prayer, followed by some questions and activities. Begin by reading the day's Scripture once or twice, allowing it to sink in to your mind and heart. Then read the written reflection for the day. The reflection ends with a simple prayer. Feel free to let this prayer begin a longer prayer and a quiet time to listen to God.

After each daily devotion, you'll find a series of questions and activities designed to engage your head, heart, and hands.

The questions help you consider how the Scripture and reading intersect with your life. This is a chance for you to hear what God is saying to you in that moment.

The activities present several options for spending time with God around the theme of treasure. We've tried to include a variety of practices, because different people connect with God in different ways. Choose one or two practices each day. Some of these may seem odd to you at first. Give them a chance! You may be surprised how God moves through these activities. See below for a list of icons used in these activities and what each represents.

As we spend time this season thinking, discussing, acting, and praying about treasure, my hope is that our conflicted and empty hearts will find their true home in God.

ICON GUIDE

THINK

NATURE

REFLECT

CREATE

DO

WRITE

GO

READ

Week One
Where Is Your Treasure?

"Stop collecting treasures for your own benefit on earth, where moth and rust eat them and where thieves break in and steal them. Instead, collect treasures for yourselves in heaven, where moth and rust don't eat them and where thieves don't break in and steal them. Where your treasure is, there your heart will be also." (Matthew 6:19-21)

1. Redefining Treasure

"Stop collecting treasures for your own benefit on earth, where moth and rust eat them and where thieves break in and steal them." (Matthew 6:19)

The first time it happened, I didn't know what she was up to.

I had come to home to visit my parents, and as I was leaving, my mom stopped me and handed me a box. It was an old cardboard box that was heavy in my arms. When I opened the box, I realized what she was doing. She was cleaning out her closets. This became her custom for the next couple of years. Every time I left, she would hand me another old box. The boxes were filled to the brim with stuff. It was my stuff.

When I opened the boxes, memories would flood over me. One box was filled with all my old trophies. Soccer, baseball, basketball, and pinewood derby trophies reminded me of my pursuits when I was younger. Another box held my baseball card collection, the one I pored over hour after hour in elementary school. Another box had photos, another notes and cards, another local newspaper clippings with my name highlighted.

My mother had given me the treasure from my first eighteen years. Surprisingly, it all fit into four or five boxes. Not so surprisingly, the stuff that had been cluttering her closet now clutters mine.

We all have stuff. We have so much stuff that our homes can't hold it all. But this book won't be an indictment on stuff. In fact, much of our stuff is quite helpful. The couches, the refrigerator, the beds all go to good use. Even the things we think that are worth keeping in boxes can hold special meaning. What I've learned, though, is that those things are not our treasure.

Jesus said we should stop collecting treasures for our own benefit. His words imply that our lives have a higher purpose than acquiring things to fill rooms and closets. This may seem obvious, until we consider where we spend the majority of our time. If most of our time is spent making money to pay for our stuff, then we at least need to pause for a moment and consider Jesus' admonition.

Stop collecting treasures for your own benefit on earth.

Jesus is not condemning stuff. Most of us need a couch, a refrigerator, a bed. Most of us are grateful for reminders of the past kept in boxes. Instead, Jesus is pointing us to a greater purpose for our lives than accumulating things in the temporary homes we live in. He has more for you.

Jesus wants to redefine what means treasure to you.

O God, I know that you have something to say to me today. Help me to hear your voice above all the noise in my life. I search after many things; help me to search for you. I have sought treasure in many places; remind me that my treasure is in you. In Jesus' name. Amen.

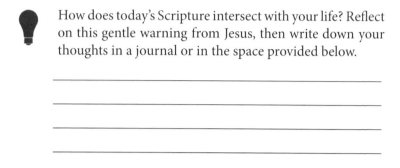

How does today's Scripture intersect with your life? Reflect on this gentle warning from Jesus, then write down your thoughts in a journal or in the space provided below.

_____

_____

_____

_____

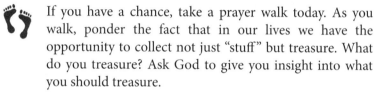

If you have a chance, take a prayer walk today. As you walk, ponder the fact that in our lives we have the opportunity to collect not just "stuff" but treasure. What do you treasure? Ask God to give you insight into what you should treasure.

Do you have any collections? What might your collection or valuables say about how you spend your time, energy, and resources?

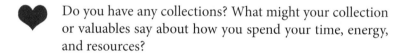

Consider taking some time to look through keepsakes you have saved over the years. Ask yourself why you saved these particular treasures, and recall what memories or reminders they hold for you.

2. The Truly Valuable

"Instead, collect treasures for yourselves in heaven, where moth and rust don't eat them and where thieves don't break in and steal them." (Matthew 6:20)

I have the opportunity to spend time with people during their last days on earth. It is one of the privileges afforded to pastors. We stand with family members when we know the end is near. We sit next to bedsides and have conversation, prayer, and tears.

I'll never forget being with John in his last few hours. I sat by the window next to his bed. As he spoke, the afternoon sunlight danced across his face. John had been one of my mentors in the faith. He had a fifty-year head start on me in the ministry, but he treated me as an equal. John talked to me about the events he remembered in his life, the things he was thankful for, the moments he regretted, the times he treasured. John talked about his family, his friends, and his God.

With John and all the others, I can't ever recall a time in those last moments when they wanted to talk about the things they had acquired on earth. No one has ever mentioned a beach house or fancy car. Rarely do folks share personal accomplishments or business ventures that went well. These things have their time and place to be celebrated, but it is not usually in the final moments.

People in their last moments talk about their family, their friends, and their God. Deathbed conversations focus on children who have been taught, mission trips that have been taken, and relationships that have lasted. People talk about vacations and moments of great laughter and surprise. They share stories that are amusing and meaningful. They talk about tragedies overcome and healing in the midst of pain. There is less talk about salaries and more about promises—promises shared with God and with people.

I'm not sure I know exactly what Jesus meant when he talked about treasures in heaven, but I think it may have been these things. Treasures in heaven come from loving God and loving people. Moth and rust can't touch these things; thieves can find no way to steal them.

Jesus was trying to move us from focusing on the temporal to keeping an eye on the eternal. Each day there are opportunities to love and serve in ways that point people to our great God. Let's be looking for those opportunities today.

God, thank you for the gift of today and the treasure that is found in it. Give me eyes to see what is truly important. Help me not to linger on the trivial, so I can grasp the valuable things you are placing before me. In Jesus' name. Amen

After reflecting on today's Scripture, consider your true treasures. What greater treasures exist in life? What do you hold dear that will not rust and cannot be stolen?

_____

_____

_____

_____

What do you think Jesus means when he refers to treasures in heaven? What does the phrase mean to you? What could it mean to you?

Consider what you might reflect on when your life is coming to an end. Are there people whom you would want to tell that you love deeply? As part of your devotion to God today, seek out one of those people and speak encouragement, love, and value.

Make a list of people and things that are your treasures. Throughout the day, remember to say thank you to God and to them. Consider handwriting a thank-you note to a special person in your life and dropping it in the mail.

_____

_____

_____

_____

3. Life Is More than Stuff

> Then Jesus said to them, "Watch out! Guard yourself against all kinds of greed. After all, one's life isn't determined by one's possessions, even when someone is very wealthy." (Luke 12:15)

When Jesus talks about treasure, he means more than just money; he is referring to how we invest our lives. Our treasure is found in the ways we spend our time, energy, thoughts, and emotions.

Clearly, though, Jesus also is talking about money. Though it makes us uncomfortable at times to talk about money in a church context, Jesus did not seem to have this aversion. He discussed money openly and often. Jesus talked more about money than he did about heaven and hell combined. Eleven of thirty-nine parables were about money. One of every seven verses in the book of Luke has some connection to money. Jesus talked more about money than anything, it seems, except the kingdom of God.

Found in Jesus' conversations about money and possessions are warnings against greed. There seems to be a natural tendency to want more, and when we get more to want even more. Today there are cultural messages telling us we are defined by what we have acquired and how high we have risen economically. Jesus says, "Watch out! Guard yourself against all kinds of greed. After all, one's life isn't determined by one's possessions" (Luke 12:15).

When we focus on what we can acquire, we focus less on God. When more and better possessions motivate us, we are motivated less by what God wants for us. Jesus warns against greed, because he knows that it leads us farther away from God.

What motivates us? What moves us? These things tell us about our hearts. Jesus cares about our hearts. After warning about greed in this passage from Luke, he tells a story of a man who acquired more and more and more. The greedy man's only consideration as he attained more was how to store it. He tore down old smaller barns and built new bigger ones. Instead of considering how these possessions might honor God and help care for others, the man only wondered how he could hold onto it longer.

Jesus warns against this type of greed, because our lives are not all about us. What we have is always connected to our relationship with God and with others. We may not be wealthy enough to need storage barns for all of our stuff, but we all have a tendency to hold on to it tightly. Jesus reminds us that our life is not found in these things. Our life is found in him.

Jesus, help me today to hear your warning about greed. I know I have the tendency to want more even when I have enough. Let my life not be distracted by earthly pursuits, so that I can see clearly how you want me to invest my time, energy, and resources. Amen.

If your life's value is not determined by your possessions, how is it determined? What makes you truly wealthy—family, friends, community, talents, gifts, experiences? Take a moment to write down ways in which your wealth is determined.

_____

_____

_____

_____

_____

As you go about your day, consider whether you ever feel resentful toward those who may have more than you. Why do you feel that way? What might you do about it?

When we hear Jesus' strong admonitions, sometimes we feel the sting of guilt or helplessness. Light a candle outdoors, in your home, or in your office today. Let the candlelight remind you that Jesus is always with you, no matter where you are. He cares deeply for all of us and only warns us because he loves us. Allowing his light into our life helps us to shine more brightly.

Find a way to share your gifts this week. As you share, try to do so not from a sense of duty but out of joy. Create and share something you love! Consider sharing your wealth through a song, a poem, a piece of art, or a delicious meal.

4. A Matter of the Heart

> Now when Jesus saw the crowds, he went up a mountain.
> He sat down and his disciples came to him. He taught them,
> saying. . . (Matthew 5:1-2)

Jesus talked a lot about money. We have established that. But why?

The Sermon on the Mount is the longest continuous stretch of Jesus' words that we have. We are told that when Jesus saw a large crowd one day he sat down on a mountainside and taught the people. What follows in Matthew 5–7 is what we have named the Sermon on the Mount.

There is a feeling at the beginning of the sermon that when such a great crowd of people needed to hear the word of God, Jesus just couldn't keep walking. He felt compelled to stop and teach. The Sermon on the Mount, though it addresses many different subjects (from anger to prayer to worry), is clearly focused on one thing: Jesus is looking at the heart.

Jesus cares about the hearts of God's people. He talks about outward expressions versus inward emotions. For example, he mentions the outward act of murder but is just as concerned about the anger in the heart that leads to murder. That anger also leads to hurtful words against our brothers and sisters, as well as to other outward expressions of what is in the heart. Again and again, Jesus looks on the inside. He longs for the transformation of our hearts, knowing that unless our hearts are changed, our actions will remain misguided and hurtful.

Jesus talks about treasure, because he knows it affects our hearts. Money does not just stay in a wallet or a bank account.

Money causes stress in our marriages. It causes division in and among people. Money and its pursuit can be all-consuming and burdensome. Those who have lost their job, for example, will tell you that it isn't just a financial issue, but an emotional and spiritual one. Jesus talked about money not because he wanted people to give their money to him or the church. There is no evidence of that. Jesus talked about money because he knew that the way we view and use our money can give our hearts great joy or great grief.

Sometimes you or I avoid difficult subjects because they might make someone feel uncomfortable. Jesus loves us too much to do that. He cares about our hearts, so he talks about the things that affect our hearts. He talks about anger and prayer and worry . . . and money. He loves us so much that he won't ignore the things that affect our hearts in a deep way.

Jesus, thank you for addressing issues of the heart. My heart is crying out for you. I need your peace, your joy, and your hope. By your Spirit, bring about change inside me so my life will look different on the outside. Amen.

If Jesus were to sit down and speak with you today, what would he say? Could you imagine talking with Jesus about matters of your own heart, including how you spend your time, energy, and resources?

_____

_____

_____

_____

What does it mean to you that Jesus risks making you feel uncomfortable by discussing things that really matter? Are there things you need to talk about with Jesus that you have been holding back?

If you had been in the crowd listening to Jesus, what issues of the heart would you have wanted Jesus to speak about? Take some time to list those issues here or in a journal.

_____

_____

_____

_____

Make time to read the entire Sermon on the Mount (Matthew 5–7) to discover what Jesus is saying to you. Some believe this is the best sermon ever preached. Consider how it applies to you today.

5. Heart Follows Treasure

"Where your treasure is, there your heart will be also."
(Matthew 6:21)

When Jesus utters these words, he forever changes the way we look at the investment of our time, energy, and money. We usually think, "Where my heart is, there my treasure will be also." In other words, the things I value and hold dear will determine where I spend my time, energy, and money. If you want to know what I treasure, then you need only to look at my heart.

Jesus says the opposite is true. You will learn about my heart by looking at my treasure. This is not just a change in semantics. Jesus knows that where our money is going will shape what is in our heart, whether we want it to or not. Financial commitments require our time and energy, and they pull our heart in directions that perhaps neither we nor God ever intended. If you buy a car that requires a significant percentage of your income, you have no choice but to spend time, energy, and money paying for it. You put your treasure into it, and your heart will follow.

If you look at where you invest your treasure now and want to change but see no easy way out, there is hope. Maybe you can attend financial classes being offered at your church or in your community. Maybe you can meet with financial experts to discuss steps to get out of a mess. Change won't be easy, but it will be worth it.

Jesus cares about your heart. Jesus longs for your heart to be at peace and wants you to invest your life in the things of God. This knowledge gives us hope that, with Jesus' help, we can make things right when investing our time, energy, and resources.

Imagine living a life in which those investments match up with our heart's desire! Imagine a time when our heart and treasure are unified in their focus. A first step is acknowledging before God that we need help. A second step is asking God to give us the desire to lay up treasure in heaven instead of treasure for us. We can do that today.

O God, I need help. For too long I have pursued the things that would give me acclaim and prestige. I have sought earthly treasure, and it has left me wanting. Give me the desire and the courage to live a life that lays up treasure for you. Give me the contentment that is only found in that pursuit. In Jesus' name. Amen.

Do you feel comfortable with the things you currently are treating as treasure? Is there some reevaluating of treasure that this Scripture could help you reflect on today?

_____

_____

_____

_____

_____

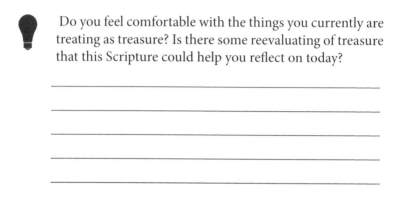 You might feel discouraged when looking at your current reality. Remember, though, that you are connected to the God who can do anything! In that knowledge, use your creative abilities to draw, paint, sculpt, sing, write, or create something that represents your dreams for the future.

 Take an initial step toward financial freedom. Research the opportunities and resources in your community for help with financial matters. Sign up for a class, go see a counselor, or borrow a book.

 Take five minutes alone today in a park, on a trail, or in your own backyard. Observe the animals around you while you are alone outdoors. What are their treasures, and what could you learn from them?

6. Eyes to See

"The eye is the lamp of the body. Therefore, if your eye is healthy, your whole body will be full of light." (Matthew 6:22)

I was headed to the airport recently for a three-day conference. It was a Thursday morning, and I was walking through our living room toward the garage to leave. Lydia, my five-year-old daughter, came running down the stairs carrying a suitcase filled with clothes, stuffed animals, and books. She said, "I'm going to the conference." I explained to her that it would be painfully boring for her. In fact, I was speaking twice, and I was sure she didn't want to hear me talk. She said, "I'll be good. I'll be quiet. I just want to be with you."

As I left, I felt a disconnect between my heart and my treasure. In that moment I valued Lydia above almost everything else, certainly above the conference, but I was going anyway. Now, most likely I will continue to attend conferences from time to time. But someday, when my life is near its end, will I wish that I had talked at more conferences? Or will I wish that I had spent more time with Lydia?

All of us have to earn money and do things we don't like to do. All of us spend time doing things we don't value as highly but that put food on the table and provide us and our families with the things we need. Within this reality, though, we can still ask ourselves, "Where am I laying up treasure?" Is it on earth? Is it in heaven?

In the middle of the passage on treasure and money in the Sermon on the Mount, there is a strange verse. It is today's

Scripture, Matthew 6:22. In it Jesus says, "The eye is the lamp of the body. Therefore, if your eye is healthy, your whole body will be full of light."

We know that the eye is what allows us to see. We also are told that if our eye is healthy, it will bring light into the body. I think Jesus is talking here about our responsibility to see and discern what is good and right. We see with our eye, and we decide whether or not to honor God. We can choose treasure that is earthly or heavenly. When we discern well and choose to honor God, light is brought into our whole being.

Part of this twenty-eight-day devotional journey is about seeing our lives and deciding how to invest our time, energy, and resources. Today our practices will center on asking God to help us discern who and what to choose.

God, each day holds options and opportunities. There are many different things that I can do and many different places I can go. Give me eyes to see the holy in the midst of the ordinary. Help me not to do things if it means I will miss the things that you truly treasure. In Jesus' name. Amen.

Does today's Scripture help you better determine where and how to spend your time and resources? If so, how?

_____

_____

_____

_____

_____

 As you reflect on today's Scripture, ask God to help you better discern the areas in which you struggle to choose where to spend your time, energy, and money, as well as what to do about them.

 Find a quiet place in nature today where you can think more about light in your life and in the world. As you enjoy the natural light and the way it comes through the trees and warms your body, consider what it might mean for you to have God's light in you. What difference would that make? Who would notice?

An ordinary sack lunch or cup of coffee can be holy time. Pick up the phone, send an email, or send a text today and make time to connect with a friend, family member, or mentor who shines the light of God on your life.

7. Heart Alignment

> I don't know what I'm doing, because I don't do what I want
> to do. Instead, I do the thing that I hate. (Romans 7:15)

Today's devotion will provide space for you to answer two important questions. The answers to these questions will be important in helping you align your heart and treasure. Rather than feeling the disconnect we have talked about, you may begin to feel the joy and peace that come with laying up treasure in heaven.

What do you want to invest in?
If you didn't have the debt or the commitments you have, what would you want to invest in? If you had no restrictions in choosing where you would spend your time, energy, and resources, where would you invest?

_____

_____

_____

_____

_____

What are you currently investing in?
Where are you spending time, energy, and money? Two good indicators are your calendar and your checkbook. When you look at your calendar for this week, where are you spending the majority of your time? With whom are you spending it? When you look at where your money is going, what are your major areas

of investment? Which areas would you like to see increased? Decreased? When you feel tired at the end of the day, where does it feel as if you've spent your energy? On what efforts? Use the space below to record your answers.

_____

_____

_____

_____

_____

Jesus tells us we can have treasure in heaven. He would not have told us this if it were not possible. So, even if change feels impossible, we should always remember that with Jesus a different reality is possible. Some of us may need to start small in thinking how we can move toward better alignment between heart and treasure. Others may be ready for a big step in making that change.

O God, thank you for caring not just about what I do, but who I am. Thank you for not only looking at my actions but looking at my heart. I want my treasure to be in you. Give me the courage and confidence to live for you. In Jesus' name. Amen.

Week Two
The Problem with Two Masters

"No one can serve two masters. Either you will hate the one and love the other, or you will be loyal to the one and have contempt for the other. You cannot serve God and wealth." (Matthew 6:24)

8. A House Divided

"If a kingdom is divided against itself, that kingdom cannot stand. And if a house is divided against itself, that house will not be able to stand." (Mark 3:24-25 NRSV)

Most Americans think of Abraham Lincoln when they hear the phrase "a house divided." Lincoln, indeed, made the phrase famous in 1858 when he spoke of a nation divided around the issue of slavery. What many don't know is that Lincoln was quoting Jesus.

Lincoln was talking about a nation that would surely fall if division remained. Jesus was talking about the certainty that a heart, if divided, would suffer greatly and would not be able to stand. In our focus verse for the week we hear Jesus give a similar warning when he talks about the difficulty in serving two masters. He says, "Either you will hate the one and love the other, or you will be loyal to the one and have contempt for the other." Jesus' next sentence, "You cannot serve God and wealth," sounds a lot like "A house divided against itself will not be able to stand."

We already have begun to consider what we are giving our hearts to and what we are investing our lives in. Today will be another day of examination as we reflect upon the divisions in our hearts. Lincoln began his 1858 speech with these words: "If we could just know where we are and whither we appear to be tending, we could all better judge of what to do, and how to do it."[1] Lincoln was analyzing the state of the union: Where were we and which way were we heading? He said that we could better judge what to do and how to do it if we accurately understood the state of our current division.

In the same way, we must understand the divisions within us if we want to invest our lives in God's treasure. Sometimes, though, we don't see that we are headed toward disaster. We don't see it coming, because we don't take time to consider "whither we are tending."

Often when people find themselves in financial disarray, for example, they realize they have been heading in that direction for some time. The problem is that they have been trying to appease more than one master. To serve more than one master, Jesus says, is something that can't be done. You end up hating one and loving the other. A divided life ends up collapsing.

Jesus warns us because he knows the sure destruction in serving multiple masters, but he also knows the power found in placing your trust in just one master. We find in Jesus a trustworthy master who will not allow us to fall.

God, I acknowledge that I have a heart that is divided. Help me today to put my full trust in you. Let me not run after or rely on other gods. Let me experience the unity of heart found in a life that is solely dedicated to you. In Jesus' name. Amen.

Does today's Scripture stir any emotions about your own divided heart? Have you allowed God to be your firm foundation?

_____

_____

_____

_____

_____

Read Mark 3:20-35 NRSV, in which the "house divided" phrase is found. Jesus has been accused of being possessed by Satan. How does Jesus show in this passage that his sole allegiance is to God? What do you make of Jesus' statement about who his true mother and brothers and sisters are?

Find a quiet place to walk outside. As you walk, consider your connection to the earth. Do you feel grounded in life? Which way are you headed? If you continue in that direction, where will you end up, and how will you feel about it?

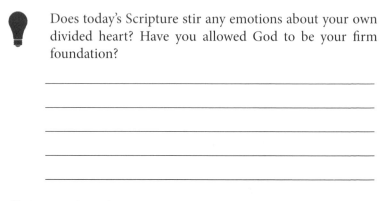

If you have access to building blocks, create a block tower alone or with a child. As you build, notice the difference in the stability of the tower when you take time to ensure the foundation is solid.

9. Every No Is a Yes

"When an unclean spirit leaves a person, it wanders through dry places looking for a place to rest. But it doesn't find any. Then it says, 'I'll go back to the house I left.' When it arrives, it finds the place vacant, cleaned up, and decorated. Then it goes and brings with it seven other spirits more evil than itself. They go in and make their home there." (Matthew 12:43-45a)

One of the reasons we have multiple masters is that we say yes too much. It's hard to say no, and we don't like to do it. We don't like to let people down. So when something is requested of us, our first inclination is to say yes. We like the initial feeling of elation that comes with it. People need us, and they are grateful. It feels good.

There are times when someone asks me to do something, and I know I should say no. I know it almost immediately. Yet I tell them I'll think about it or pray about it, because I so dislike the feeling that I'm not able to be all that others need or expect me to be. Sometimes I even say yes, though it's obvious I should say no.

Multiple yeses lead to multiple masters. Every time a yes obligates me to another commitment, I am stretched thinner and have less time for what I truly want to invest in. We must choose our yeses carefully. We must also learn that every time we say no, we have an opportunity to say yes to something else. Every no, in other words, is really a yes.

Jesus talks about how an unclean spirit that has been told no in one place wanders around looking for another resting place. The person who once was filled with a bad spirit now has an opportunity to say yes to the things of God, to say yes to that which is holy and good. If that person does not let the no lead to a yes, then the unclean spirit will return and bring with it seven other spirits more evil than itself.

Ask God to give you the courage today to say yes to the things that truly are treasure. Remember, though, that saying yes to one thing will almost certainly mean saying a very clear no to something else. It will feel uncomfortable at first, but as you learn to say no to multiple masters, you will be able to say "Yes!" to your one true Master.

God, help me to be intentional about what and whom I say yes and no to. May your Spirit guide me to an undivided life that lays up treasure in heaven. In Jesus' name. Amen.

What might this Scripture and reflection be saying to you about how you use your yeses?

_____

_____

_____

_____

Reflect on the word *no*. Say it to yourself a few times. How does it make you feel? Does the word come easily when requests are made of you, or do you feel uncomfortable saying it? Reflect in a similar way on the word *yes*. What emotions does it raise in you?

Spend some time in prayer considering to what God is calling you to say no. Make a list of the top five things you need to say no to. Likewise write the top five things that you hope to say yes to.

_____

_____

_____

_____

_____

As you go about your day, take note of the times when you say no and the times when you say yes. Before speaking or answering, say a brief prayer asking God to guide you in whether to say yes or no.

10. Unintended Masters

> Elijah approached all the people and said, "How long will you hobble back and forth between two opinions? If the LORD is God, follow God. If Baal is God, follow Baal." The people gave no answer. (1 Kings 18:21)

Elijah warned against trying to serve both God and Baal. Jesus warned about trying to serve both God and money. The options seem clear, and the right choice seems obvious. I choose the one true God, not Baal. I choose my one master, the Lord, not wealth.

However, in our lives the options and choices don't always seem so clear. We find ourselves serving masters whom we never intended to serve. We find ourselves seeking treasure that is not our heart's desire. We work overtime to pay off debt on things that give us little joy. We work so hard and so fast that sometimes I think we don't even realize that our lives are divided and we are serving multiple masters. We have unintended masters, and we don't know how to get rid of them. Like the people Elijah was addressing, we don't have a good answer when we are asked, "How long will you hobble back and forth" between multiple masters?

A first step for me is slowing down long enough to see all the directions where my life is headed. When I slow down (as you are doing right now to read this devotion), I often see something beautiful that reminds me of what I truly treasure. I pick up my guitar that's covered in dust. I get on the carpet and roll around with the kids. My wife and I have a meaningful conversation, like friends, or we just laugh together. I sit with church members and learn something unique and beautiful about them. When I do these things, I usually tell myself, "This is always around me! What am I doing that causes me to miss it?"

We have only so much heart, so much time, so many resources to go around, and when we begin serving six, seven, or eight masters that require everything of us, then our treasure sits to the side, dwindling away because we can't get to it. Then we feel like the people described in James 1:8 as "double-minded" and "unstable in all their ways."

God is calling us to a singular devotion to Jesus. How do we get there? It starts with slowing down enough to realize we have multiple masters. Our devotional exercises today will be about slowing down long enough to see the beauty that God is placing before you.

God does not desire for you to run through life giving yourself to every god that beckons. God desires you. You are God's treasure. Find your treasure in the Lord.

God, slow me down so I can see the condition of my heart. I admit that I have given myself to multiple masters. As I see you more clearly and hear your voice, allow me to let other allegiances drop away, strengthening my devotion to you. Amen.

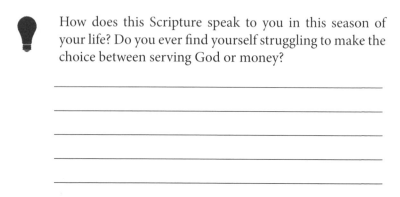

How does this Scripture speak to you in this season of your life? Do you ever find yourself struggling to make the choice between serving God or money?

_____

_____

_____

_____

_____

 Find time today to go for a walk. As you walk, slow your pace. Then slow some more. Try to be aware of what is happening around you as well as what is happening in you. As you slow your pace, try to slow down all that you are. What do you see? What do you hear?

 Carve out time in your day to enjoy God's creation. It may be through dancing, playing music, eating delicious food, watching a sunset, taking a hike, or enjoying the trees, animals, and birds. As you participate in God's greatness, be reminded that you are not in control. Remember that there is only one Lord, and that is all you need.

 Find time today for five or ten minutes of silence. Turn off your phone, computer, and television. During that time, try to clear your thoughts and simply rest in God's presence.

11. Master Jesus

> Because if you confess with your mouth "Jesus is Lord" and in your heart you have faith that God raised him from the dead, you will be saved. (Romans 10:9)

It was one of the shortest and earliest Christian confessions. It is common to hear Christians say it even today.

Jesus is Lord.

In early Christianity, this simple phrase was revolutionary and life-threatening for the confessor. To say that Jesus was Lord meant that you did not recognize the current king or Caesar as Lord. Early Christians thus put their lives on the line when they proclaimed Christ as Lord. Even if they were slaves to another person, Jesus was the true master.

As we have seen, Jesus makes it clear in his teachings that we can't serve two masters. (That means having seven or eight is out, too.) It doesn't work. We end up liking one and hating the other. I think this explains why we can get so disdainful, even hateful, about the things that pull us away from our treasure. Our job, our boss, our commitments to this and that are probably not all that bad, but we can end up despising them because they pull us away from our treasure. Does this mean we can't make money? No. Does this mean we can't have a healthy relationship with money? No.

It does mean that Jesus has to be master; God is Lord. God is actually described at times as a jealous God. God does not want to share your allegiance. God doesn't want a piece of your life or an hour a week. God wants to be everything to you.

I have a jealous wife. She has a jealous husband. We are jealous for each other's time, each other's conversation, each other's love.

If I am not giving her all that she deserves, she will let me know. Love is jealous.

When we make Jesus our master, here is the cool thing: our needs find their proper place as they flow out of our relationship with the master. The master makes all the difference in every part of your life. How good is a good job if your boss is a jerk? How much do you have to love the work if your master is a terror? There's no job that good.

Jesus is a good master. We must say, "Lord, you are everything to me. You are my treasure. I want my relationship with my family, my friends, my job, my finances all to flow and be subservient to you." If we say these things and truly mean them, then we will begin to experience the joy of having one good master. His name is Jesus.

Lord Jesus, today I confess with my mouth and believe in my heart that God raised you from the dead. This confession and belief give me life, and they color all the other parts of my life. Be the master of all I think, say, and do today. In your name. Amen.

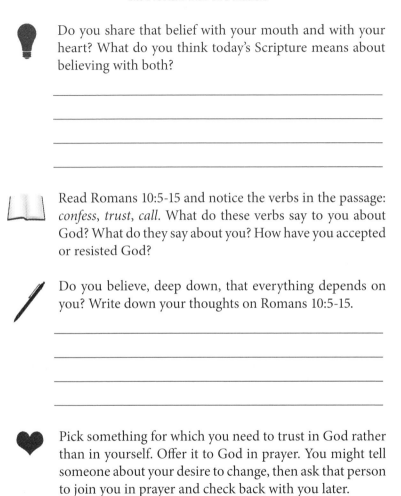

Do you share that belief with your mouth and with your heart? What do you think today's Scripture means about believing with both?

_____

_____

_____

_____

Read Romans 10:5-15 and notice the verbs in the passage: *confess, trust, call.* What do these verbs say to you about God? What do they say about you? How have you accepted or resisted God?

Do you believe, deep down, that everything depends on you? Write down your thoughts on Romans 10:5-15.

_____

_____

_____

_____

Pick something for which you need to trust in God rather than in yourself. Offer it to God in prayer. You might tell someone about your desire to change, then ask that person to join you in prayer and check back with you later.

12. Getting Rid of Gods

> Then Samuel said to the whole house of Israel, "If you are turning to the LORD with all your heart, then get rid of all the foreign gods and the Astartes you have. Set your heart on the LORD! Worship him only! Then he will deliver you from the Philistines' power." So the Israelites got rid of the Baals and the Astartes and worshipped the LORD only. (1 Samuel 7:3-4)

As we read the Bible, we should be careful to note the difference between references to *God* and *gods*. The two terms mean very different things. God is good; gods aren't good.

In today's passage from the book of 1 Samuel, for instance, the people of God had to be reminded that they were to worship only the one true God. Samuel made it clear that if Israelites were turning to the Lord, then they must get rid of all the other gods. In this story, as in many others, the people did get rid of their gods but then picked them back up a little later.

Not long ago I bought a new car—not brand new but new to me, and I really liked it. I was happy to get it. It was clean when I got it. Really clean. In fact, one of the first things I did was buy new mats to go on the floorboards. It looked even cleaner.

Just the other day, my family and I got into the car. My wife, Rachel, was up front with me, and our three girls were in back. We were headed to the park on a beautiful summer day. We stopped at a drive-through, and the girls ordered their favorite: grape Slushies. Before we pulled out of the parking lot, three-year-old Phoebe set her grape Slushy in an imaginary cup holder and let go of it. I heard the Slushy hit the floor, and my heart broke. Purple sticky goodness covered the back of the car. Immediately I became furious. I asked Phoebe, "Why did you do that?" She responded, "I don't know." We were supposed to be heading to the park on a beautiful summer day, and instead I was in a fast-food parking lot scrubbing and cleaning and muttering. None of my girls said a word, but I sensed them wondering, *When did this car become so important?*

The answer: When I made it important.

God is eternal and sometimes is called the Uncreated One; gods, though, have a maker, and it's us. When our identity becomes more wrapped up in the thing than in the one true God, we have created another god. I don't just have a clean car; I'm the clean car guy. I don't just close big deals; I'm the guy who closes big deals. I don't just love going to football games; I'm the tailgate master. When that happens, things that can be good become bad.

Where do you find your identity? If Samuel were talking to us today, perhaps he would put it this way: "If you are turning to the LORD with all your heart, then get rid of all your gods. Set your heart on the LORD! Worship him only! Then he will deliver you from your enemies' power."

The final verse, as in today's Scripture about the Israelites, would be up to us: "So we got rid of the gods and worshipped the LORD only."

God, set our hearts on you. Deliver us from the power of other gods. Give us strength to get rid of these poor substitutes and worship only you. Amen.

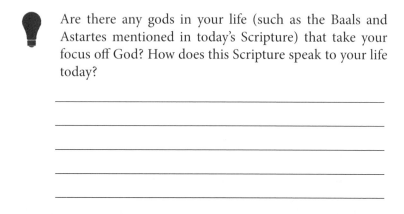

Are there any gods in your life (such as the Baals and Astartes mentioned in today's Scripture) that take your focus off God? How does this Scripture speak to your life today?

_____

_____

_____

_____

_____

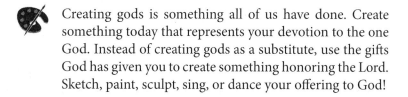

Pay attention to your conversation topics throughout this day and week. What do they reveal about other gods in your life? You may want to write down your thoughts to reflect on later.

Creating gods is something all of us have done. Create something today that represents your devotion to the one God. Instead of creating gods as a substitute, use the gifts God has given you to create something honoring the Lord. Sketch, paint, sculpt, sing, or dance your offering to God!

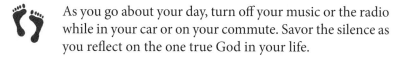

As you go about your day, turn off your music or the radio while in your car or on your commute. Savor the silence as you reflect on the one true God in your life.

13. The Difference between God and Gods

> In a violent rage Nebuchadnezzar ordered them to bring
> Shadrach, Meshach, and Abednego. They were brought
> before the king. . . . Shadrach, Meshach, and Abednego
> answered King Nebuchadnezzar: "We don't need to answer
> your question. If our God—the one we serve—is able to
> rescue us from the furnace of flaming fire and from your
> power, Your Majesty, then let him rescue us. But if he
> doesn't, know this for certain, Your Majesty: we will never
> serve your gods or worship the gold statue you've set up."
> (Daniel 3:13, 16-18)

Yesterday's devotion reminded us that we are the ones who
make gods, but the one true God made us. The creation stories
in Genesis teach us who the Creator is, and we are reminded of it
again and again throughout the Bible.

Often we think of our treasure as the things we will be able to
make, earn, or acquire during our lives. A basic shift takes place in
us when we realize that our treasure is not about what we do; it's
about who God is.

The familiar story of Shadrach, Meshach, and Abednego is
about a king who found his identity in created gods and three
men who found their identity in the Creator. When these three
faithful servants of God did not bow down to Nebuchadnezzar's
created god, this powerful king became furious with rage. He
was threatened by the faith of these humble men, because the
meaning of his life was wrapped up in the gods he had created.
We see in our own lives that our relationship with gods leads to
anger and fear.

If you find yourself experiencing a lot of anger and fear, you may want to ask yourself, *What am I giving excessive attention to?* If a grape Slushy sets you off, you may need to check your heart and see what you're giving attention to. If you can't sleep at night because of climbing interest rates, you may need to check your heart and see what you are worshiping.

A relationship with gods leads to anger and fear, and a relationship with God leads to peace and calm. This doesn't mean you'll always be floating on a cloud with no concerns in the world. It doesn't mean you won't experience anger and fear. But a relationship with God leads to peace. It is promised, and it is given. Shadrach, Meshach, and Abednego stood before a king who was furious with rage, and they experienced peace because they knew who created them. They knew God would save them; and if he didn't, they would still stand behind their decision. "Because we are not going to live like you." They were free from all the things that bound Nebuchadnezzar because of his gods.

Our gods tell us that security is found in protecting everything; God tells us that security is found in being willing to give up everything. The three servants walked into the fire, unafraid because their security did not depend on an earthly king but on their one true master.

As we examine our treasure, we will find that a relationship with God leads us to give things away, and in giving them away finds more than any god or possession could ever promise.

God, lead me away from anger and fear and the emotions that are found in serving multiple gods. Lead me toward your peace as I put my trust in you, the one true God. In Jesus' name. Amen.

The one true God saved Shadrach, Meshach, and Abednego. Describe how the one true God saved you from a situation in life.

_____

_____

_____

_____

Read the full story of Shadrach, Meshach, and Abednego in Daniel 3:1-30. What gods in our society do we feel forced to worship? What stand should we take against them? Are you willing to go into the fire for God?

Consider taking a break from electronic media for the rest of the day and going without a computer, phone, or television. Consider turning off alerts on your computer and phone for incoming emails and social media for the remainder of the week.

Create a list of gods that tempt you. In a safe way, consider burning your list in a fireplace or other controlled area. How do you feel as you watch your list of gods burn?

_____

_____

_____

_____

14. More than Lip Service

"This people honors me with their lips, but their hearts are far away from me." (Matthew 15:8)

Jesus expressed displeasure at those who give their words to God but keep their hearts to themselves. It's easy to do. Church people are the best at it. We talk a good game, but many of us close our hearts to God.

There was a time in my teenage years when I was saying most of the right words, but my heart was growing farther and farther away from God. One of the pastors at my church, who I knew could tell, came by my house one day to check in on me. I wasn't there. He left a sheet from a yellow notepad that I kept on my bedside table for years, on which he wrote these words: *He not busy being born is busy dying.*

The pastor knew I would recognize those words from a Bob Dylan song.[2] Dylan was one of my favorites and one of his. When I read the words, they pierced my heart in a way they never had before. Suddenly I saw something I hadn't seen. My heart was far from God. I was not moving closer to God; I was not even standing still. I was moving away, not with my words but with my heart.

That day, I decided to honor God not just with my lips but with my heart and my life. Somebody had cared enough not just to send me a card or pray for me, but to come into my room and write words that I could understand. He didn't care about me coming to youth group; he cared about me.

Jesus doesn't care so much about your money; he cares about you. He talks about your treasure because he treasures you. God doesn't just send a card or a message. God tried that for a while, but we didn't listen. So God chose to come to where we live, to the place we thought no one would dare come. God comes to our hearts and speaks to us in a way that we can understand.

How should you respond? Give God your heart. Not just your words or your time or your energy or your money. Give God your heart.

What are the gods in your life?

_____

_____

_____

_____

_____

What would it mean for you to serve only one master?

_____

_____

_____

_____

_____

Week Three
Giving Your Treasure Back to God

"Be careful that you don't practice your religion in front of people to draw their attention. If you do, you will have no reward from your Father who is in heaven.

"Whenever you give to the poor, don't blow your trumpet as the hypocrites do in the synagogues and in the streets so that they may get praise from people. I assure you, that's the only reward they'll get. But when you give to the poor, don't let your left hand know what your right hand is doing so that you may give to the poor in secret. Your Father who sees what you do in secret will reward you.

"When you pray, don't be like hypocrites. They love to pray standing in the synagogues and on the street corners so that people will see them. I assure you, that's the only reward they'll get. But when you pray, go to your room, shut the door, and pray to your Father who is present in that secret place. Your Father who sees what you do in secret will reward you." (Matthew 6:1-6)

15. Something Bigger than I Am

> Without losing faith, Abraham, who was nearly 100 years old, took into account his own body, which was as good as dead, and Sarah's womb, which was dead. He didn't hesitate with a lack of faith in God's promise, but he grew strong in faith and gave glory to God. He was fully convinced that God was able to do what he promised. (Romans 4:19-21)

In Romans, Paul recounts the amazing story of Abraham and Sarah. Long story short: God promises an old couple with no children that they will have as many descendants as the stars in the sky. They have a baby at the ages of 100 and 90. They give God all the credit.

Abraham trusted in God's promise. He was fully convinced that God was able to do what God had promised. It never could have happened if it had been left up to Abraham and Sarah. But it wasn't. This was God's thing all along, and God allowed them to be a part of something bigger than themselves.

This is a common theme throughout the Scriptures: God can do anything but, amazingly, chooses to involve us.

Last November, after watching a network news piece on the plight of Native American children on reservations, some folks in our church asked the question, "What can we do to help?" They didn't feel right living comfortable suburban lives while these Native American children lacked the care that is taken for granted in our community. After watching the piece and discussing it, they asked our church to pray about partnering with a community center in Clinton, Oklahoma, that cares for children in need. Since that day, our church has given tens of thousands of dollars to help. Four trips have taken place. A scholarship fund has been established. We know the children's names; they know ours. And it has only just begun.

The reason I mention that example is because my family and I made a decision about how much we might give to the efforts for these children. Our contribution was significant to my family, but not significant when set next to the larger number that was raised. The important thing was that we got to be part of it. It's a powerful thing to know that your life is playing a role in something bigger than you.

As you consider your treasure, consider what you can give to play a role in God's work. Can God do it without us? Sure. But we miss out when we withhold our treasure from the beautiful things that the people of God are doing.

God made a big promise to Abraham and Sarah, making their family a part of the great things God would do for all people. God makes the same promise to you and your family.

God, help us, like Abraham, to hear the great things you are calling us to be a part of. Give us faith like Abraham and Sarah's, that even when things seem preposterous, we will believe they are possible. Show us how to give what we have to be part of a greater work. Amen.

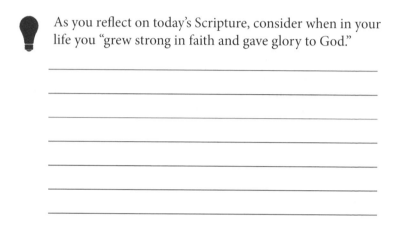

As you reflect on today's Scripture, consider when in your life you "grew strong in faith and gave glory to God."

_____

_____

_____

_____

_____

_____

_____

Are there barriers that keep you from believing you could be part of God's work? What are they, and how might you overcome them? Remember, God wants to remove those barriers and invite you into his work.

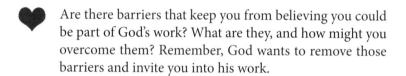

Slowly read Romans 8:28. Read it again. As you do, listen for the word or phrase that stands out for you. What is God trying to say to you today?

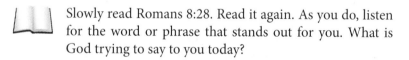

As you go about your day, find a way you can do something good for someone else. The ideas are endless.

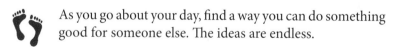

16. A Warning against Performing

"Be careful that you don't practice your religion in front of people to draw their attention. If you do, you will have no reward from your Father who is in heaven.

"Whenever you give to the poor, don't blow your trumpet as the hypocrites do in the synagogues and in the streets so that they may get praise from people. I assure you, that's the only reward they'll get. But when you give to the poor, don't let your left hand know what your right hand is doing so that you may give to the poor in secret. Your Father who sees what you do in secret will reward you." (Matthew 6:1-4)

When Jesus says "Be careful," we ought to be careful.

Usually we tell people to be careful if we think there's a good chance they might be hurt. If I tell my kids to be careful, it's usually because I see a strong possibility that what I'm warning against is about to happen. At dinner time, if I set down glasses of milk in front of two wiggling, laughing girls and say, "Be careful not to spill the milk," it's because I believe there's a high probability the milk will spill.

In today's Scripture Jesus says, "Be careful that you don't practice your religion in front of people to draw their attention." In other words, Jesus is warning us against performing. Of course, lots of performances are good, and I'm sure are ordained and approved by God. God does not approve, however, when we make a show of giving.

We are not to practice religion for the purpose of drawing attention. We are not to give to the poor in hopes that we will receive praise. And Jesus would not have warned us against this if he did not know it was likely to happen. Jesus knew that we like to draw attention to ourselves and receive praise.

As a boy, I would do a number of different things to get attention. I still do. There is a need in all of us to be recognized, to feel valued, to be noticed for doing something good. Jesus is saying in this passage that when it comes to doing things with and for God, we should be careful about the need to be noticed. When we seek recognition for doing God's work, we might get a pat on the back; but we miss out on being part of God's great work. Why? Because when we get the credit, God is forgotten; and we miss out on the amazing reward of participating in something only God can do.

When you practice your religion, don't do it in front of others. Don't blow a trumpet so people will praise you. Instead, look for ways to give God the attention, and take joy when you realize that God let you join in. Then, when people praise God, join in the praise! The reward will be so much greater than a pat on the back.

O God, so often I clamor for attention. I want people to notice me when I do things for you. Give to me the humility of Jesus, who always pointed people to you and to the great things that only you can do. Give me the joy that comes from simply playing a part in what you are doing. In Jesus' name. Amen.

What do these words mean to you? "Your Father who sees what you do in secret will reward you." Reflect on today's Scripture and take note of anything it brings to mind in your own life.

_____

_____

_____

_____

_____

_____

_____

 Find a quiet place where you can be alone outdoors. Breathe the air deeply. Trust that God is as close to you as your breath.

 Before you begin your work, studies, or chores today, light a candle and place it in your workspace or on your desk as a reminder that God is with you and that you offer all that you are to the glory of God.

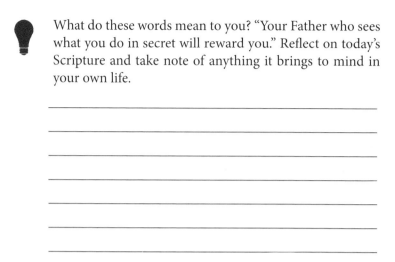 Pray Psalm 91. As you pray each verse, be reminded of how much we truly are reliant on God.

17. Praying and Giving

"When you pray, don't be like hypocrites. They love to pray standing in the synagogues and on the street corners so that people will see them. I assure you, that's the only reward they'll get." (Matthew 6:5)

In a passage largely about giving, money, and treasure, Jesus makes an abrupt change and talks about prayer. This does not mean, however, that Jesus has gotten sidetracked. Instead, he is linking the two together. It turns out there is a close connection between giving our treasure away and living a life committed to prayer.

Jesus says that our prayer should be like our giving. Don't pray on the street corner or pray to get attention. Rather, do it quietly, because prayer is about connecting with God, not impressing people. Now, praying to get attention isn't a big problem for most of us. Many times we would rather not pray in front of people. But in other religious activities, most of us do have a tendency to put the focus on ourselves. We are tempted to show people how religious we are and how good we are. When we do this, we may gain attention; but we may also miss out on connecting with God.

As a pastor, I pray in front of people all the time. I pray in church, in the hospital room, before the meal—you name it. Sometimes people will joke and say, "You're the professional; you pray!" At these times I feel somewhat uncomfortable, being typecast as the religious one in the group. Clearly, Jesus was not big on folks' getting attention for grandiose prayers. The reward, it seems, was in the quiet, humble prayer.

This isn't to say public, corporate prayer is not important. In fact, praying together is very important. We must remember, though, the spirit in which we bring our prayers to God. For me, my biggest day of public prayer is Sunday. This is the day when I am before the most people, oftentimes being called on to pray. The most meaningful Sunday prayer for me, though, happens earlier in the day. It happens when I kneel next to my bed before I leave for church, when the children are asleep and the sun not yet up. My wife grabs my hand and prays quietly over me for the coming day. That is when I feel closest to God. The reward of the quiet prayer is great.

Jesus knows that prayer is most effective when we are quietly drawn into the presence of God, not when we are getting attention for our adept articulation of theological truths. Quiet, humble prayer leads us to give everything we have. That is why Jesus links praying and giving. The closer we come to God, the less value earthly treasure seems to hold.

God, draw us near to you in prayer. We pray not to gain attention from others but to give our attention to you. As we come near, compel us to give and give generously. In Jesus' name. Amen.

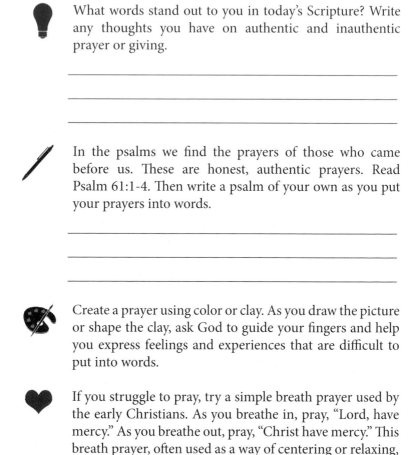

What words stand out to you in today's Scripture? Write any thoughts you have on authentic and inauthentic prayer or giving.

_____

_____

_____

In the psalms we find the prayers of those who came before us. These are honest, authentic prayers. Read Psalm 61:1-4. Then write a psalm of your own as you put your prayers into words.

_____

_____

_____

Create a prayer using color or clay. As you draw the picture or shape the clay, ask God to guide your fingers and help you express feelings and experiences that are difficult to put into words.

If you struggle to pray, try a simple breath prayer used by the early Christians. As you breathe in, pray, "Lord, have mercy." As you breathe out, pray, "Christ have mercy." This breath prayer, often used as a way of centering or relaxing, can also serve as a cry for help. Is a parent or colleague struggling with the loss of a job? *Lord, have mercy.* Is a friend moving away? *Christ, have mercy.* Even when we can't find the words to pray, we still can draw near to God.

18. Don't Walk Away Sad

Jesus said, "If you want to be complete, go, sell what you own, and give the money to the poor. Then you will have treasure in heaven. And come follow me."

But when the young man heard this, he went away saddened, because he had many possessions. (Matthew 19:21-22)

When I was twenty years old I went to Rio Bravo, Mexico, for the first time. Up until that point, most of my life had been about me.

That week, I was part of a construction team building a new home for a working-class family. We built an attractive block home that doubled the size of the lean-to they had been living in. The owner of the new house, Victor, was a man who provided for his family by selling produce from his garden. Each morning he would leave early on a bicycle that had makeshift baskets on it filled with vegetables. He would ride a couple of miles to town and sell the vegetables for a handful of coins. This life provided most of what the family needed.

Victor had a two-year-old daughter named Cecilia. Cecilia first stole, then broke, then changed my heart. I began spending the late afternoons playing with her. These days, as the veteran dad of three girls, these sessions seem like no big deal; but for a twenty-year-old college student it was a new and captivating experience. We would play, then she would fall asleep in my arms as I rocked her and sang to her. I sang a portion of an old Simon and Garfunkel tune: "Cecilia, you're breaking my heart, you're shaking my confidence daily."[3]

When I first saw her family's possessions, I thought, "This family has nothing." By the time we had been there a week, I realized that the family had everything. They laughed harder, sang louder, worshiped more passionately, and hugged tighter than I did. It was as if the absence of possessions made them better at living. At age twenty, I realized that by the world's standards I was already a rich man, and yet I had much to learn from Cecilia and her family about living, giving, and being connected to God.

Jesus said that it is hard for the rich to enter the kingdom of heaven. We have so much that gets in our way. Possessions and wealth don't necessarily cause sadness, but they do when we choose them over the things of God. Jesus tells us to give our earthly treasures away and in so doing find the heavenly treasures that are right before us.

What is standing in your way?

My experience with Cecilia changed the way I looked at treasure. The possessions I was striving for paled in comparison with the life-giving things we miss in our scramble for the next dollar, the next award, the next accolade. I came to realize that treasure could be found in things such as laughter and dancing and hugging and playing.

If you are like me and tend to go so fast that you are missing out on life, remember Cecilia and examine your treasure.

God, help me see the things that stand in the way of living and giving. What have I made into treasure that I need to give to you? Speak to my heart today so that I won't have to walk away sad. In Jesus' name. Amen.

What emotion does this Scripture evoke for you? Be honest with yourself, then write your response below.

_____

_____

_____

_____

Recall the events of yesterday or today and review them as if you were watching a movie. Where did you see God? How did God speak to you?

Take a few moments to write down some of the people and things that make you feel truly alive. Then write down some of the people and things that drain you. Are there things you can give away that would lead you closer to a life in God?

_____

_____

_____

_____

 Find time today to clean out a closet or empty a drawer. Consider letting go of some things that may no longer be important or necessary.

19. The Blessing of Enough

> Bring the whole tenth-part to the storage house
> so there might be food in my house.
>> Please test me in this,
> says the LORD of heavenly forces.
> See whether I do not open all the windows of the heavens for you
>> and empty out a blessing until there is enough.
> (Malachi 3:10)

After my experience in Mexico as a young man, I knew that I couldn't continue living my life in the same way. One of the things that I felt compelled to do was to give. I realized that following Jesus had a direct connection to giving, though I didn't know what or to whom. I began to look for ways in which I could give my time, energy, and money to honor God. A month after leaving Mexico, I became engaged to Rachel; and we prayed about our how our lives might not just be about us but be involved in the things God considers treasure.

One evening while Rachel and I were eating dinner with an older couple from our church, they shared with us how tithing held great meaning for them. Of course, I had heard of tithing or giving ten percent, but I had never experienced an adult conversation about it. The couple told us they found great freedom and joy in giving away their money. In fact, they had recently made a decision to give one percent more each year, in hopes of one day giving away the majority of their income. Rachel and I decided that night to tithe and, like the couple, to strive each year to give away more and more. It wasn't hard at first, because we didn't make much money!

But as we have made more and given more, the commitment truly has given us freedom and joy.

In today's Scripture, God says, "Test me in this." If we believe God to be trustworthy, then we should take the test. For some of us it will mean giving for the first time, while for others it may mean giving more than ten percent.

God goes on to say, "See whether I do not open all the windows of the heavens for you / and empty out a blessing until there is enough." *Enough*—that is what we really need. Not more, not a lot, but enough.

The way to find enough is not in storing up things for ourselves, but in giving to God first to demonstrate our trust and confidence. When we give to God, we are reminded that God is our source, the one who truly takes care of us. When we hold back, we put the burden and pressure firmly on our own shoulders. This leads to anxiety and unrest.

Is God calling you to give, to tithe, or to give more than a tithe? There is a blessing waiting for you.

God, we don't want to hold back any longer. Help us to trust you as we give you what is yours. The faithful act reminds us that you are in charge and that you desire to bless us. Amen.

In what ways has God poured out blessings on your life? Review today's Scripture to discover what other words and phrases stand out to you today.

_____

_____

_____

_____

_____

_____

Read 1 Kings 19:5-9a. Tired and hungry, Elijah fell asleep—twice. In what ways do you identify with Elijah? For what things do you need to rely on God? For what things do you hunger and thirst?

As you eat lunch or take a break today, give thanks for the many ways God cares for you and provides for you.

Start a gratitude journal. Begin by listing at least five blessings that God has poured out on your life today. Revisit this practice daily or weekly, and watch your list grow.

_____

_____

_____

_____

_____

20. Getting Caught Up in the Confetti

So, whether you eat or drink or whatever you do, you should do it all for God's glory. (1 Corinthians 10:31)

As mentioned previously, Jesus teaches in Matthew 6 that giving and praying are not about us getting attention. Everyone likes recognition, and there is nothing wrong with that; but the purpose of giving and praying—and really of life itself—should not be getting personal recognition but giving glory to God. The things we do and say are to show others who God is. As Paul says in today's Scripture, we "should do it all for God's glory." The one who should get recognition is God! God's name and renown should be the desire of our hearts.

I am reminded of what happens on the playing field after a championship has been won. The air is filled with the celebratory sounds and fluttering confetti. There are a few people being recognized on a small stage—maybe the coach, the owner, and a star player—but everyone feels a part of it. This includes the players who never made it onto the field, the equipment managers, the families who traveled miles to attend. These people are not concerned about who is and isn't being recognized. Instead, there is a feeling of gratitude just to be there and be included.

The great things that happen in this life will ultimately not be accomplished because of us. God is the one who does great things. But we get to be a part! We stand in the confetti and witness the beautiful things that only God can do. God gets the place on the stage. God gets the credit. God gets the glory. That is as it should be. Yet, what a wonderful thing that God lets us be included.

Our hope to be included in the things of God should affect the ways we give and pray and live. Whatever we do, it should be done for God's glory.

If we were honest today, how many of the things that we do are focused on us? How many of our investments have God's glory in mind?

Jesus assures us that the greatest rewards are found in humble, quiet devotion to God—devotion that is done not to garner praise but only to honor God.

God, thank you for letting us join in what you are doing! We are so grateful to stand alongside as you get all the glory. Our participation means more than any personal acclaim we could receive. Help us to live and give in such a way that our lives give you credit! Amen.

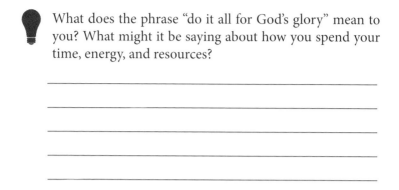

What does the phrase "do it all for God's glory" mean to you? What might it be saying about how you spend your time, energy, and resources?

_____

_____

_____

_____

_____

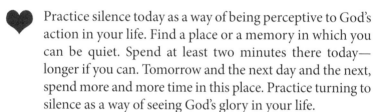

Practice silence today as a way of being perceptive to God's action in your life. Find a place or a memory in which you can be quiet. Spend at least two minutes there today— longer if you can. Tomorrow and the next day and the next, spend more and more time in this place. Practice turning to silence as a way of seeing God's glory in your life.

The constant distractions of technology often cause us to miss out on hearing what God says. Leave your cell phone or tablet at home, and head outdoors. Listen to the sounds of creation around you. Listen for the sounds of silence. Listen for the voice of God.

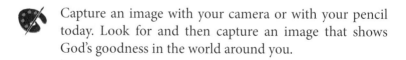

Capture an image with your camera or with your pencil today. Look for and then capture an image that shows God's goodness in the world around you.

21. Life as Prayer

"But when you pray, go to your room, shut the door, and pray to your Father who is present in that secret place. Your Father who sees what you do in secret will reward you." (Matthew 6:6)

We have seen that Jesus links giving and praying. We don't make financial decisions independent from our prayer life. We don't give just to do what is right or help those in need; we do it in devotion and obedience to God.

Today's devotion will provide space for you to think and pray about how to incorporate prayer into your life. As you consider what God has been saying to you about your treasure, remember that financial decisions are done in relationship with God. They are not purely about responsibility or obligation. They are not about inducing guilt or placing yet another burden on you. Giving is a way of responding to God for the great things God has done. Giving is our answer to God's invitation to join Jesus in his mission.

Read 1 Kings 19:11-13. Elijah heard God's voice, not in the thundering sounds of earthquake, wind, or fire, but in the "sound of sheer silence" (NRSV). How do you expect God to speak to you? Continue our emphasis from yesterday's devotion in setting aside silent time to listen and be present with God.

Write a prayer to God. Reflect upon what God has been saying to you during the past three weeks. Be honest with God about the feelings and emotions you have felt in response.

_____

_____

_____

_____

_____

Turn your life into a prayer. Wherever you are, whatever you're doing, be aware of God's presence. Try these ideas:

Keep a Bible or picture of Jesus on your desk, backpack, or purse. Wear a cross or hang one in your car. Let these symbols remind you to be in conversation with God.

Each day, as you move from one activity to the next, offer your day to God by praying: "God, hold me close to your heart."

Choose one day each week to spend intentionally in God's presence. Throughout that day, try to keep up an ongoing conversation with God. Ask for guidance as you make choices or decide how to react to situations. If you let the conversation lag, don't give up. Talk with God about your mistake, then pick up where you left off.

Find ways to put your prayers into action.

Meet with a friend to discuss how God is calling you to invest your life. Study and pray together. Hold each other accountable to the changes you decide to make.

Make a financial commitment to the church so you can join in the great things God is doing through the church.

Create "bags of grace" containing nonperishable food items, a bottle of water, personal hygiene items, a prayer card, and information on social service agencies in your area. Keep one or two in your car to give to needy people you encounter.

Volunteer at a local school, food agency, or community service.

Week Four
Don't Worry 'Bout a Thing

"Therefore, I say to you, don't worry about your life, what you'll eat or what you'll drink, or about your body, what you'll wear. Isn't life more than food and the body more than clothes? Look at the birds in the sky. They don't sow seed or harvest grain or gather crops into barns. Yet your heavenly Father feeds them. Aren't you worth much more than they are? Who among you by worrying can add a single moment to your life? And why do you worry about clothes? Notice how the lilies in the field grow. They don't wear themselves out with work, and they don't spin cloth. But I say to you that even Solomon in all of his splendor wasn't dressed like one of these. If God dresses grass in the field so beautifully, even though it's alive today and tomorrow it's thrown into the furnace, won't God do much more for you, you people of weak faith? Therefore, don't worry and say, 'What are we going to eat?' or 'What are we going to drink?' or 'What are we going to wear?' Gentiles long for all these things. Your heavenly Father knows that you need them. Instead, desire first and foremost God's kingdom and God's righteousness, and all these things will be given to you as well. Therefore, stop worrying about tomorrow, because tomorrow will worry about itself. Each day has enough trouble of its own." (Matthew 6:25-34)

22. What to Do with Worry

"Therefore, I say to you, don't worry about your life, what you'll eat or what you'll drink, or about your body, what you'll wear. Isn't life more than food and the body more than clothes?" (Matthew 6:25)

Worry can be defined as being anxious or uneasy about something uncertain or potentially dangerous. With that definition in mind, we can see that not all worry is bad. Some worry can be quite helpful, since it serves as a survival mechanism that keeps us out of trouble. Usually, though, when we talk about worry, we are referring to that irrational, purpose-lacking, unhelpful stream of thoughts that plagues us rather than protects us, that hinders us rather than helps us. Worrying may grow out of an innate instinct for survival, but it can grow into a destructive force rather than a life-giving emotion.

Referring to this destructive force, Jesus tells us in today's Scripture, "Don't worry." He even names some of the things that usually cause us worry, such as food and drink and clothes. For many of us, these basic needs are taken care of through our work, and the work itself causes us worry.

It is no accident that Jesus discusses worry right after talking about treasure and money. He knows that our need to make money produces anxiety. I did a very unscientific study with my friends on Facebook by asking them, "What do you worry about?" The constant themes in their responses were family, finances, future, and how those three things fit together. For example, people said they were worried about "this crazy world and what I have got my kids into" and about "being a mother, wife, teacher, all in one." In other words, they weren't worried about just one of those things; they were worried about all three things. It made me wonder: How do we juggle all the things we are doing, needing, seeking?

Jesus says, "Don't worry."

It's easy for him to say. What does Jesus know about facing economic instability, debt ceilings, and fiscal cliffs? Of course, just about the time we ask that question, we remember that what we are facing is not new. We are not the first generation to fear for our future, just the latest generation. The people Jesus talked to on that hillside experienced the same emotions we do. He told them, "Don't worry." He tells us, "Don't worry."

Life is more than food, and the body is more than clothes. Jesus, after all, is concerned not with material things, but with our hearts. When our treasure is in God, all those other things (family, finances, future) fall into their rightful place, a place beneath God in our allegiance and attention.

This week, we will explore how to trust God with the things that cause us to worry and how to find the peace Jesus gives to anxious hearts.

Jesus, I often worry about things I shouldn't. I think I am in control of things that are really out of my control. Help me to hear you say, "Don't worry" and to put my trust in you. Send your peace to me today. I pray in your name. Amen.

We know that life is more than food and clothing yet the basic necessities of life have a way of making their way to the top of the importance list. How does this Scripture speak to your life today? What about life stands out to you as important right now?

_____

_____

_____

_____

_____

 What things are you worried about today? Take a moment to lift those things up to God. Speak them slowly and directly to God.

 During the day, take your Bible outside and read aloud the Creation story found in Genesis 1:1-31; or at night, go outside with a flashlight and read aloud Psalm 8. Consider the power of a God who creates just by speaking.

 Make time today for exercise. Consider a walk, run, bike ride, dance class, or yoga class. As you move, release any physical stress that may be weighing you down.

23. Look at the Birds

"Look at the birds in the sky. They don't sow seed or harvest grain or gather crops into barns. Yet your heavenly Father feeds them. Aren't you worth much more than they are?" (Matthew 6:26)

Jesus tells those listening to his Sermon on the Mount to look at the birds. When the hearers do so, he reminds them that birds are fed and taken care of by God. Then he asks them, "Aren't you worth much more than they are?"

Well, aren't you?

While sitting in a meeting recently, I heard United Methodist Pastor Jorge Acevedo remind a group of clergy that everyone we encounter is a child of God and person of worth. Many times, though, we are not sure if we are even as valuable as birds. This is not to say that birds aren't valuable; in fact, they are so valuable that they don't have to sow seed or harvest grain or gather crops. God just takes care of them. Birds are valuable; but to God, you and I are more valuable.

Do you believe that?

The same point is made in the Bob Marley song which, perhaps not coincidentally, is called "Three Little Birds."[4] Marley sings,

Don't worry about a thing,
'Cause every little thing gonna be all right.

In Marley's song, birds remind him there is no need to worry, because everything is going to be all right. Jesus says much the same thing in the Sermon on the Mount. How can we know this?

We are children of God and hold great worth to the one who can provide our every need.

O God, sometimes I forget that I am of great worth to you. I pay attention to voices that tell me I am something less than a child of God. Remind me of the value that I hold in your eyes. Help me to live as one who holds inestimable worth as a member of your family. Amen.

How does this Scripture encourage your worth today? Do you feel worthy? Why or why not?

_____

_____

_____

_____

_____

Read Matthew 6:25-34. Do you feel less than a child of God? What voices, thoughts, emotions, or experiences have led you to this place? Bring your insecurity and self-worth to God, and hear Jesus pronounce the sacred worth that belongs to all children of God, including you.

Take special care today to notice birds. What do you feel God is saying to you through the presence of birds in your life? Purchase some bird seed or toss some bread scraps out for the birds, and notice their response.

Write yourself a love note from God. What would God say to you about your worth and how much you are loved?

_____

_____

_____

_____

_____

24. Don't Worry, Be Happy

"Who among you by worrying can add a single moment to your life?" (Matthew 6:27)

In the Sermon on the Mount, Jesus' "don't worry" song continues with some practical advice. In his question, shown in our Scripture today, Jesus' implication is clear. What does worry gain us? Does it solve our problems? Does it give us more time? The simple and irrefutable answer to Jesus' question is that we don't add a moment of time to our lives by worrying. In fact, we lose precious time by doing so. However, just because we know logically that we shouldn't worry doesn't mean we won't worry.

We mentioned one "don't worry" song in our meditation yesterday. Today we'll give you another one, a famous pop song by Bobby McFerrin.[5] The song reached number one on the pop charts in 1988. Here are a couple of lines:

In every life we have some trouble . . .
Don't worry, be happy.

The mantra is one most of us long to adopt. The sentiment is easy to connect with; we all want a more carefree, worry-free, happy existence. Of course, it is more easily said than done.

In the Sermon on the Mount, is Jesus simply saying, "Don't worry, be happy"? Not exactly. Jesus isn't suggesting that we can talk ourselves out of anxiety or into happiness. He isn't saying to use logic and move on. Instead, he is pointing us toward the root cause of most worry: we think that ultimately we are in control. We think that time and life are dependent on us.

Jesus tells us not to worry and points us to our God, who truly holds time and life. Worrying will not add a moment to your life. Trusting in God, though, will allow you to embrace the time that God has given you here.

God, remind me that true peace is found in relationship with you, rather than in pushing for contentment. I cannot add a single moment to my life by worrying, so I choose to trust you so that I might truly live. In Jesus' name. Amen.

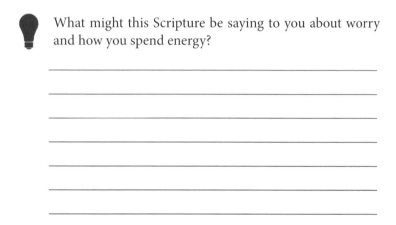

What might this Scripture be saying to you about worry and how you spend energy?

_____

_____

_____

_____

_____

_____

_____

What would it be like for you to do what the songs say and not worry as you go about your day today? What does happiness mean to you, and how can you move toward achieving it in your everyday life?

Use a concordance or search online to find five Scriptures that include these key words: *worry, anxiety, peace, trust.* Write the words on separate strips of paper, and put them in places that will be visible to you throughout the day (such as on a bedside table, mirror, dashboard, or desk). Notice how the words speak to you differently in different moments in the day.

Write a simple poem or song releasing your worries to God.

25. A Different Perspective

"And why do you worry about clothes? Notice how the lilies in the field grow. They don't wear themselves out with work, and they don't spin cloth. But I say to you that even Solomon in all of his splendor wasn't dressed like one of these. If God dresses grass in the field so beautifully, even though it's alive today and tomorrow it's thrown into the furnace, won't God do much more for you, you people of weak faith?" (Matthew 6:28-30)

As Jesus continues his "don't worry" song in the Sermon on the Mount, he suggests that we notice the flowers. Flowers don't wear themselves out with work; they don't spin cloth for their clothes. God dresses the flowers beautifully. God cares for them. As with Jesus' example of birds, he points to the lilies to give us a different perspective.

Jesus wants us to notice beautiful things that God created and that God cares for. When we move quickly through our life, we may not notice the birds; but with God's perspective we see them, with their beauty and their value. God puts within the birds the instinctive desire to move to places of better climate and more provision when it is time. Jesus says, "God feeds the birds; they are of worth to God, and you are of more worth." You are God's treasure.

Similarly, Jesus wants us to notice the lilies of the field. We pass by flowers as we move place to place. With God's perspective, we see their beauty and their value. Jesus says, "God dresses the flowers in the field. God takes care of them. God will take care of us." Once again, Jesus is saying that we are God's treasure.

Does this mean that those who trust in God don't have to work? I don't think so. Jesus is saying that we are valuable to God. He knows there will inevitably be times when we worry about what we will eat and what we will wear. He is reminding us that we are God's creation and that God cares for us and will take care of us. Jesus' images of birds and lilies give us perspective on how God looks at us.

We do a daily devotional. We join a faith community for worship. We make prayer a pattern of life because we need God's perspective. Jesus sang a "don't worry" song over those gathered on the hillside to remind them that God wants to give all that we need and to be all that we need. We are God's treasure, and we find our treasure in Jesus.

So often, God, we see what we want to see. Give me your perspective today to recognize the beautiful things you have created and be reminded that I am a part of them. When I feel unworthy today, remind me that I am treasure to you. When I seek the things of this world, remind me that my treasure is found in you. Amen.

What are some ways this Scripture encourages you to continue growing in your faith?

_____

_____

_____

_____

_____

Today write down some of the things you see that God created. For each thing you notice, write down any insights or perspectives you have gained simply by noticing them.

_____

_____

_____

_____

_____

Draw or paint a picture that represents the creation. Include yourself or something that represents to remind you that you are a part of God's creation.

Today, plant some seeds that are appropriate to the season. Care for them, and let your daily attention to the seeds give you perspective on how God views and values you.

26. God Knows What You Need

> "Therefore, don't worry and say, 'What are we going to eat?' or 'What are we going to drink?' or 'What are we going to wear?' Gentiles long for all these things. Your heavenly Father knows that you need them." (Matthew 6:31-32)

After the birth of our first child, I was amazed, overwhelmed, exhausted . . . and worried. My wife, Rachel, and I were able to hold our daughter Mary for a few moments, then were told she would be taken to the nursery for cleanup, measurements, and tests. I said no.

I couldn't imagine handing my new daughter to strangers. My anxiety would not allow me to let her out of my sight. The nurses explained that this was normal procedure and assured me that our baby would be safe. Still seeing my reluctance, they invited me to walk with them to the nursery. The nurses and I rolled Mary down the hallway together, and after arriving at the nursery door they explained what Mary would experience over the next couple of hours. They said, "You can return to your room now, Mr. Armstrong." I said no.

The nurses laughed nervously. My persistence was amusing and annoying at the same time. They invited me into the nursery and put me in a chair next to the little bed where Mary was warmed under hot lights. As I sat there, I realized I was being watched by families on the other side of the glass who had come to see their new offspring. People peered in to see the babies, and there was a new father who hadn't shaved or slept in two days and was trembling with fear.

I had my phone in my pocket, and at that moment I felt the buzzing of a new voicemail. It was my friend Tommy. His message was short and simple. He said, "Jacob, God is in control of that little girl. Her every breath in and every breath out are not your responsibility. Starting today, you have to entrust her to the God who knows everything she needs." It was as if Tommy had been standing outside the glass, watching me. (I found out later that he had!) I stood up, looked at that little baby, and walked out of the nursery.

Life is uncertain. It is dangerous and wild. Worry will come. When we look at our greatest treasure, we will feel anxious about caring for it. But Jesus says that we don't have to worry, because God knows everything we need. As a new father, I did not know all that Mary needed or all that I needed in order to care for her. My friend's voicemail reminded me that God knew, and that was enough. The knowledge that God knows and cares can sustain us through times of uncertainty and fear.

As you consider your greatest treasure and what is needed to care for it, remember this: Your heavenly Father knows what you need.

God, thank you that you know what I need, even when I don't. Help me to entrust my treasure to you, knowing that you will care for it. In Jesus' name. Amen.

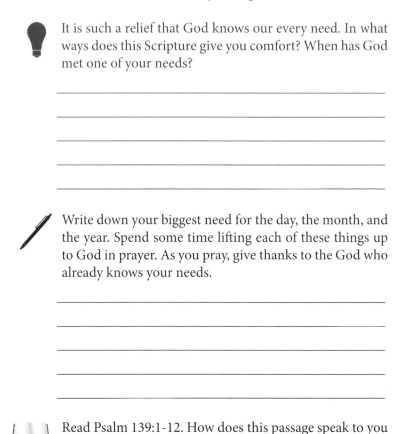

It is such a relief that God knows our every need. In what ways does this Scripture give you comfort? When has God met one of your needs?

_____

_____

_____

_____

_____

Write down your biggest need for the day, the month, and the year. Spend some time lifting each of these things up to God in prayer. As you pray, give thanks to the God who already knows your needs.

_____

_____

_____

_____

_____

Read Psalm 139:1-12. How does this passage speak to you of God's understanding and care for your needs?

Consider your community of faith. How has being part of that community met your needs over the years? Spend time in silent reflection thanking God for the times that our needs are met through community.

27. First and Foremost

> "Instead, desire first and foremost God's kingdom and God's righteousness, and all these things will be given to you as well. Therefore, stop worrying about tomorrow, because tomorrow will worry about itself. Each day has enough trouble of its own." (Matthew 6:33-34)

Every day we are given the task of trusting God with the people and things that are most important to us—our treasure. We also trust God for what we will eat, drink, wear, and need. As we have learned this week in Jesus' Sermon on the Mount, we become worried when we try to maintain complete control of our treasure and take sole responsibility for our needs. Notice that Jesus does not say we are exempt from hard work and obligation; we simply need to acknowledge that our part in the job is minor and that, ultimately, these things are in God's control and not ours.

We are to desire "first and foremost God's kingdom and God's righteousness," and our needs will be met as well. Jesus recognizes that there are other things in our lives that demand our attention and cause us concern. He recognizes their importance. He just wants to help us understand the proper place that each of these things should hold in our hearts.

First and foremost in our hearts should be the things of God. In much the same way that our greatest commandment is to love God, Jesus says our greatest pursuit should be after God's kingdom and God's righteousness. When the things of God become what we truly treasure, we find that the other things we have valued do not demand as much from our hearts. As we give our hearts more and more to God, our treasure is more and more in God and not in the things of this world.

Even as Jesus tells us not to worry, he warns us that "each day has enough trouble of its own." He tells us to let tomorrow worry about itself. As we face the trouble of this day, our desire for God's kingdom and righteousness causes our worry to fade. As we learn more and more about the treasures of God, we put less and less stock in the treasures of the earth. We begin to invest our time, energy, and money into the things of God; and we find freedom from the things that used to hold us in the grip of worry and fear.

Today, God, I seek you first. Before I look to the things I have to care for and the people I have to provide for, I seek you. I desire your kingdom here on earth. I desire your righteousness instead of trying to create my own. I seek you first and experience the joy of all the other things you have given me. In Jesus' name. Amen.

How does this Scripture encourage you to face your tomorrows? What might it be saying to you about how you spend your time, energy, and resources on a daily basis?

_____

_____

_____

_____

_____

Make a list of some things you think God would have you seek. Make a second list of some things you are tempted to seek first. Compare the lists and reflect on what they mean.

_____

_____

_____

_____

_____

What are you concerned about that could be included in what Jesus called "worrying about tomorrow"? In prayer, offer your worries into the care of the God who holds tomorrow.

Watch a sunrise or sunset, and give thanks for another one tomorrow.

28. Finding Treasure in God

"Where your treasure is, there your heart will be also."
(Matthew 6:21)

What have the past twenty-eight days meant to you? Was there a certain week, day, question, or activity that stands out in your memory? How will you look at treasure differently? What new steps can you take to find your treasure in God? Spend some time writing about your experience.

_____

_____

_____

_____

_____

_____

_____

_____

_____

_____

_____

_____

_____

_____

Notes

1. Lincoln, Abraham. "A House Divided." Speech, Springfield, Illinois, June 16, 1858. American Rhetoric. http://www.americanrhetoric.com/speeches/abrahamlincolnhousedivided.htm.

2. Dylan, Bob. "It's Alright Ma (I'm Only Bleeding)" (Song Lyrics). Accessed February 17, 2014. http://www.azlyrics.com/lyrics/bobdylan/itsalrightmaimonlybleeding.html.

3. Simon, Paul. "Cecilia" (Song Lyrics). Accessed February 17, 2014. http://www.lyricsfreak.com/s/simon+and+garfunkel/cecilia_20124635.html.

4. Marley, Bob. "Three Little Birds" (Song Lyrics). Accessed February 17, 2014. http://www.azlyrics.com/lyrics/bobmarley/threelittlebirds.html.

5. McFerrin, Bobby. "Don't Worry, Be Happy" (Song Lyrics). Accessed February 17, 2014. http://www.azlyrics.com/lyrics/bobbymcferrin/dontworrybehappy.html.